JEZEBEL'S GOT THE BLUES
...AND OTHER WORKS
OF IMAGINATION

Jezebel's Got the Blues

JEZEBEL'S GOT THE BLUES...
AND OTHER WORKS OF IMAGINATION

by

Merrill Farnsworth

A Collection of Monologues and Dialogues
Inspired by the Old Testament,
Told with a Southern Voice and Tinged with the Blues

SILVER BIRCH PRESS
LOS ANGELES, CALIFORNIA

ISBN-13: 978-0615653501

ISBN-10: 0615653502

Email: silver@silverbirchpress.com

Web: silverbirchpress.com

Mailing Address:
Silver Birch Press
P.O. Box 29458
Los Angeles, CA 90029

INQUIRIES FROM PRODUCERS: To license this work for a staged reading or theatrical presentation, please contact Merrill Farnsworth at her website: writingcircle.org.

PURCHASING COPIES IN QUANTITY: To purchase copies of this book for an approved staged reading or theatrical presentation, send an email to silver@silverbirchpress.com for ordering information.

JEZEBEL THANKS ALL WHO HAD A HAND
IN BRINGING HER TO LIFE.
This long list includes early encouragers,
steadfast mentors,
amazing friends,
talented actors,
Silver Birch Press,
and especially one bluesman
who said yes to improvising *The Persian Blues*.

TABLE OF CONTENTS

The pre-show playlist includes songs written or performed by Mahalia Jackson, Blind Willie Johnson, and others. During the performance, improvised blues melodies drift in and out of the readings. Stories are not presented in proper chronological order, but in proper "Jezebel order"...she hopes your imagination enjoys the ride.

Art and Soul Studio, Nashville, Tennessee

Author's Note

Jezebel's Got the Blues...is a collection of stories and paintings created over a nine-month period. As an artist, I often go into the studio, take up a brush filled with paint and begin making marks on paper or canvas, letting the marks take shape and allowing shapes to emerge, as they will. One day in September, a face began forming and I followed the inclination to form a woman's face. In time, I saw the face of Jezebel staring out at me, and it occurred to me she looked frightened. I'd always imagined her as defiant.

As a daughter of the South, I was warned about Jezebel and picked up on the notion she was a bad apple. I was told she wore too much rouge and knew she came to a bad end. Having gone through a period of life that didn't end so well, I felt a certain compassion for Jezebel when she showed up that day in September. I began painting more and more layers of red on her cheeks, thinking that somehow more red would keep her from feeling so blue. As I painted, I began imagining a story about Jezebel, told from the point of view of the rouge on her cheeks – a voice that became a strange witness to her story.

That is how a series of stories and paintings came to be called *Jezebel's Got the Blues...and Other Works of Imagination*. After I finished the paintings and had written the stories, I called upon friends, all talented actors I'd performed with over the years. I asked if they'd join me to perform this series of monologues and dialogues. All said yes, as did Phil Madeira, who accompanied us with improvised blues on his guitar. It was a magical night for me. All my imagining became something real – to me, my friends, and to the audience gathered for the retelling of stories about a ragtag crew of characters who share a longing for grace to bend the notes of our blues towards love.

I pay tribute to the voice of Flannery O'Connor, whose prose I hear as hard-edged, satirical, and yet loving towards the hapless, wayward subjects of her fiction. Also to Tennessee Williams – his lyrical voice lends dignity to even the most tragic of his characters.

The set consists of stools for the actors and, if possible, images of the paintings originally created for this work. The paintings are individually set on an easel as each story is told, with the cast members changing out the paintings according to the story being told. Actors are dressed in black shirts and jeans.

ANGEL AT EDEN'S GATE

ANGEL AT EDEN'S GATE

CHARACTERS:

Angel

*Serpent (**bold** text)*

I am the angel at Eden's gate. I knew them, the man and the woman. I knew them before they knew what God only knows. I knew them when they strolled through the garden with effortless grace, lips curved gently upward, eyes shining with morning light. Paradise was their playground and God was their friend. They fed one another grapes of impossibly purple hue and drank nectar from fragrant flowers. I knew them when they romped playfully with a lion, loved with abandon, body and soul tangled in unfettered bliss. I stood unseen at the gates of Eden, a silent witness.

I was there when the serpent knocked.

Hello, Angel.

He was long and lean, leading with his belly, thinking to slide on by.

Sworn to guard the entrance to Eden, I blocked the way and ordered him gone without discussion. He smiled, lipless and dry, with no intention of leaving.

Move aside, sister. Paradise is mine.

His cool stare chilled the air, but when he spoke his voice was warm, delicious, golden. He both delighted and disgusted me. I felt myself craving the sweet poison of his intoxicating tone.

The all-knowing God does not smite me, reject me, or dismiss me. Dear angel, how could I even exist if not for God's hand? Let me in. All God's creatures belong in the garden.

I was tempted, but not fatally. I was without choice to be persuaded by any will but my Lord's. I was created to guard this holy gate. I would not be moved. It was the serpent that moved, slowly and surely. He was now so close that the strange icy heat of his breath was upon my brow.

Let...me...in.

How long we stood there face to face I cannot tell you. What I will confess is that I could have stood there forever locked in the dark rapture of his topaz eyes. What I will further confess is that if God had not appeared at that moment, I might have allowed the serpent into paradise. I did not. It was God who let him in.

I was ordered to step aside as the serpent entered paradise.

Poor Angel...so...innocent.

I had assumed the garden was perfect without this disturbing creature. I would have sent him away. Better yet, I would have destroyed him...

Silly Angel...don't you know God prefers stories that are...complicated?

I watched the serpent weave silently among the trees when the moon was full. He favored a tree laden with golden fruit. The woman had eyes for this tree. She knew it was extraordinary, but was perfectly content to let it be – *perfectly content* until the day the serpent's voice wrapped itself all around her.

The fruit of this tree is delicious. More delicious than anything you've ever tasted. It will melt on your tongue like the sweetest honey, dripping from the honeycomb.

I watched her face as she listened to his words. There came a certain light to her eyes. A certain tilt to her head.

Just reach out your hand…pluck it. It's easy.

Remembering God did not want her near this tree, she ran. But at that moment, the fruit of the tree entered her dreams and upon waking she was drawn to its branches. The serpent was there to greet her.

Just one bite. It will be our secret.

The woman, she had no concept of "secrets"… but the word, as he whispered it slowly, began to rise in her like a wave. The ground beneath her feet was no longer steady. She became confused and began wondering why, exactly why, the fruit was forbidden. As the serpent guessed her thoughts, more of his words washed over her.

Eat from this tree and you will know good from evil. You will be like God. You will see beyond the walls of Eden. Don't you want to see? Don't you want to know all there is to know?

She had never considered knowing all there was to know, but now, the world beyond paradise entered her imagination. I was in tragic awe of the questions that began growing in her mind, a mind sewn with the seeds of God's own imagination.

Just take one bite…

She did. The man, he took a bite too. The fruit, sweet in the mouth of God, was bitter in theirs. In an instant, they hated their bodies. I saw them hiding in the tall grass as first blood spilled on the ground, blood of a creature slain to clothe their shame. I saw the serpent cursed, cast down on his belly, topaz eyes trapped in the body of a worm. To my great joy, God banished this venomous tempter from the garden forever.

I know you don't weep for me, but be melancholy Angel, for the man and the woman – they're following me out into the big bad world. And you know why...because God said so.

So the story of the woman and the man strolling through the garden with effortless grace now ends. As they pass through the gates of Eden, I see their faces reflected in the flame of God's eyes.

They are fierce. They know sorrow. They are beautiful.

THE MARK

THE MARK

CHARACTERS:

Man

*Woman (**bold** text)*

NOTE: *This piece bestows a blessing on the Cain in all of us. The last line is spoken in unison.*

Every beginning finds an end…

…every ending finds a new beginning. This story begins outside Eden's gates with the birth of a son…

… then another, two brothers, Cain and Abel…

…one brother ending the life of the other in a jealous rage. Feeling the sting of rejection, Cain cut into his own flesh and blood…

…killed what he loved and tried to bury the shame, but God witnessed the crime.

The story could have ended with Cain cold in the ground next to Abel, struck down for murder. Instead God sent Cain to wander the earth in search of a new beginning...

...just as we all must seek new beginnings when we kill what we love.

On his journey, Cain received The Mark, a mark to protect him from all those anxious to give him what they thought he deserved.

This Mark is for all who have killed...

...be it hope or joy
justice or mercy
tenderness or trust
time or tomorrow or today.

Comfort or peace
thankfulness or rest
the yearnings of the child within
the caresses of your lover's arms.

This Mark is for all who have cut...

…your billowing sails,
before journey's end,
the blossom of a promise,
reaching towards light.

The roots of your soul,
the wings of your spirit,
the cords of kinship,
the bonds of a friendship.

This Mark is for all who have murdered…

…a vision, a vow, or a dream,
the flight of imagination,
or the landing of love,
in your heart.

Your calling, your talents,
the meaning of your story,
your belief in beyond,
the sparkle in your eyes.

This Mark is for all who have buried…

...secrets or shame,

disappointment or desire,

your kinship with the dark,

your passion for the rising of the dawn.

Your laughter, your longing,

your innocence, your wonder,

your impulse to play,

to sing, to fly, **to dance.**

For all who wander in search of life and love...

...take the Mark of Cain,

a sign of grace to protect the prodigal,

until he finds,

until she finds,

PEACE.

I AM THE RAT

I Am The Rat

CHARACTER:

Rat

NOTE: *This rat is very pleased with himself.*

I am the rat on Noah's ark, one of two to be exact. When me and the missus showed up, Noah's wife looked at us as if we were getting ready to spread the plague right then and there. What made her all high and mighty? Who was she to judge whether or not we should be saved? It's not our fault we didn't get to be bunnies or kittens.

The day I got the call from on high, I was busy gnawing on some dead guy's toe. It was a big toe, nice and juicy. Sorry. Noah's been teaching us social skills, so I'm aware this sort of talk is offensive. Deep breath. Just forget I mentioned it. Like I was saying, I got a message from above.

This is the way I remember hearing it: *World to end SOON. Get your rat's anatomy down to Noah's Ark NOW. Take Mrs. Rat with you.* I said to myself – *that hussy?* She ran off with a river rat years ago. Wasn't sure what happened to her when all the rivers dried up. Didn't care. Not having a current missus, I went out to find Noah on my own.

Noah was a favorite topic of conversation in that cozy little den of iniquity I called home. He'd stand outside preaching and yelling about a giant flood washing away every sinner on earth. Everyone laughed, but to my thinking those gypsies, tramps, and thieves should have been at least a little worried. They were the sinningest of sinners. They lived filthy lives, which I totally supported; but if I'd made the mistake of creating them, I'd want a do-over.

And if I were Noah, I'd want a new wife. That woman's high strung – goes hysterical every time she sees me.

Those night crawlers back in the city didn't flinch at the sight of my beady eyes or long pink tail. It was like they were begging me to hang out. It was like a dream...rotting food all over the floor, the stench of human misery hovering in every corner. Just thinking about it makes me homesick.

Now I'm stuck here with a crazy woman who keeps trying to scrub away the stink of the place. I swear she tried to sweep me overboard. If my dear missus hadn't pinned my tail between her pointy teeth and heaved me back on deck, I'd have been down at the bottom of the sea with all the other rats. That's right. The missus and me are back together.

You might look at her and go – really? God called her? She curses like a sailor – something she picked up from her river rat – drinks and smokes, too. She's been forced to give up her filthy habits since coming here, but I guarantee she'll backslide the minute she gets half the chance. That's my woman. But, hey – did she even think to find me when she got the call? No.

She tried talking some other loser into making the trek. Not that I thought to look for her, either; but at least I didn't try to bring another rat to the party.

It really messes with my mind to think we're the only two rats left on earth. What's the meaning of this? The wife says don't worry about it, but I can't help wondering. I'm deeper than she is – more sensitive. Can you believe that after all those years apart we found each other again? There I was, following that voice I heard telling me to go find Noah and then – out of nowhere – there she was. I thought I'd want to kill her if I ever saw her again, but instead I said to myself: *We're both rats, she's my rat, let's do this.*

Me and my second-chance mama scurried our way down to the ark with all the other prancing, scuttling, waddling crew…all us creatures climbing on board a boat with no vacancy for the folks who, by the way, quit laughing at Noah when raindrops big as jungle cats pinned them to the ground.

And there I was, the lowliest of creatures, rising above the rich and strong; and there was Noah, the man they'd been calling a fool, looking down at them from the deck of his boat. Every man, woman, and child cried out to him for mercy; but mercy wasn't up to Noah, it was up to God, and God was done with these people. They'd had their chance. They'd disappointed him. Now they were sinking to the bottom of the ocean, gasping for air that was no longer theirs to breathe.

Even I, a rat, felt sorry when they saw it was over and slid silently into a dark, wet grave. At what point does the world become so wicked it deserves death? I don't know. All I know is that I can't wait for the rain to stop. I can't wait to get off this boat. I can't wait to get back to the business of being a rat.

THE KISS

THE KISS

CHARACTER:

The Kiss of God

NOTE: *This piece is about the original desperate housewife, looking for something more…*

Every woman desires a kiss, long and hard, given to her by someone who knows every secret, every whim, every mistake she's ever made, someone who knows everything and still loves her. I am that kiss, God's kiss on the lips of a woman with no name.

The woman is Lot's wife and people know more about her husband than they want to know – for instance his sons were also his grandsons. *(A CAST MEMBER TWANGS OUT A FEW NOTES FROM "DUELING BANJOS," A SONG FROM THE MOVIE DELIVERANCE)* Think about it – it's not good.

All that is really known about Lot's wife is that she turned to salt. Why? Gossips say she left a lover in Gomorrah and was petrified to see him go up in flames. Legalists say she disobeyed God's command to keep her eyes on the path ahead was punished for looking back. Skeptics say that if she existed at all, she didn't run fast enough and was trapped by lava.

But I know a secret. Lot's wife got exactly what she wanted.

She'd always wanted to be special. While her brothers and sisters were running around, mindlessly sprouting into wildflowers, cedar trees, and stubborn weeds, she sat down and crowned herself "The Rose of Canaan."

Her mother wanted her learn to weave or gather herbs, but what her mother wanted wasn't good enough. She wanted to marry a rich man, so she seduced a man named Lot who owned a lot of livestock.

Marriage was not as special as she'd expected, so she imagined giving birth to a great prophet or a future king – but no sons for her, only daughters.

One day, Lot announced they were moving to the Jordan Valley. When they were captured along the way, Lot's wife fantasized the evil, but handsome, king would take her into his harem, demanding all Lot's livestock as ransom. The king never looked her way.

Years later, when the story of their capture was written down, Lot's wife was listed as one of the household possessions, not as The Rose of Canaan, or by any other name. She began to feel old and invisible. Her husband and daughters seemed bored with her. She was bored with herself. Life was dull.

Then Lot brought home "the visitors." He didn't bother to introduce her to them. She would have liked for the guests to know her name.

How long had it been since her husband, or anyone else had spoken her name? She couldn't remember. Lot's wife was at peace with being forgotten, but she longed for a glance from the visitors, who were so strangely beautiful that they'd attracted an unruly mob. Lot knew what the crowd wanted and shouted out:

Don't do this wicked thing! Look, I have two daughters. You can have them, but don't do anything to these men, for they are my guests.

Before Lot's wife could protest, the visitors took charge. They pulled Lot back into the house and blinded the mob so they couldn't find the door. She heard the two beautiful men speaking urgently to her husband.

Save your sons and daughters! Get them out of here because we are going to destroy this place.

No mention of saving a wife. A hot burst of shame shot through her belly. She knew this pain – this begging to be looked at, to be entered into, this desperate desire to be known – to be loved for the selfish, shallow girl she had been, for the lost, lonely woman she'd become, a longing to be poured out of her cold shell of body into a warm embrace.

Lot's wife sat down and waited for the end to come.

An angel came at dawn, taking her hand, forcing her to run from the house. Another angel shouted out a warning to her husband: "Don't look back, for if you do, God will turn you to salt."

And what of her? Would the God of heaven and earth bother to turn Lot's wife into salt? Would he even notice if looked she back?

Still feeling the angel's touch on her hand, she ran, following her husband and daughters as fire fell from heaven.

What would hurt more, she wondered, *to look back and feel her body turning stone cold or to look back and feel nothing?*

Lot's wife was sick of feeling "nothing." Suddenly, the courage to risk everything opened up her heart like a perfect rose, and she turned to face the fire – feeling my kiss on her lips, warm and deep as God called out her name, lifting her from the cold shell of her body into Love's embrace.

A CONVERSATION WITH DOUBT & DEFIANCE

A Conversation with Doubt & Defiance

Characters:

Spirit of Doubt (Sarah)

Spirit of Defiance (Hagar)

NOTE: *As in all of the readings, look for humor where you can find it, even if it is dark.*

DOUBT: I am Doubt.

DEFIANCE: I am Defiance.

DOUBT: Sarah's Doubt.

DEFIANCE: Hagar's Defiance.

DOUBT: Double trouble.

DEFIANCE: Double divine.

DOUBT: Double down –

DEFIANCE: …and dirty.

DOUBT: When innocence dies, when questions arise, when faith grows impatient.

DEFIANCE: When enough is enough, when there's nothing to lose, when faith is broken and shattered in pieces on the ground – reduced to laughter. *(SHE TURNS TOWARD DOUBT)* You know what I'm talking about.

DOUBT: I assume you're referring to Sarah's moment of hilarity when the God of Abraham told her she'd birth a son when she was nearly one hundred years old.

DEFIANCE: What the hell were you thinking? Making her laugh at God wasn't a good idea.

DOUBT: Hey! If God didn't want the woman to laugh, he could have arranged for a more dignified delivery date.

DEFIANCE: The world's messed up, and it's your fault.

DOUBT: Ha! My fault? You're the one who encouraged Hagar to rebel.

DEFIANCE: That's because you turned Sarah into a paranoid tyrant.

DOUBT: That would have never happened if you hadn't come along and ruined that little Egyptian girl's sweet nature.

DEFIANCE: You mean compliant nature.

DOUBT: Exactly! Sarah and Hagar had such fun together back when Hagar knew her place.

DEFIANCE: Sarah had the fun – Hagar fetched and fanned.

DOUBT: Hagar had it good. Even though she was a servant girl, Sarah treated her like family.

DEFIANCE: As long as Hagar did as she was told.

DOUBT: Admit it – Hagar was thrilled when I planted my little seeds of doubt in Sarah's mind and convinced her that the only sure way to get a son was to arrange for her husband to sleep with "the help."

DEFIANCE: Thrilled? What choice did Hagar have but to obey Sarah's orders?

DOUBT: Really? You – Defiance Incarnate are suggesting Hagar had no choice? Why didn't you convince that concubine to run away, to refuse to do Sarah's bidding – or to kill herself, if necessary?

DEFIANCE: Are you kidding? I knew it would turn out well for Hagar to become Abraham's wife. It made her Sarah's equal.

DOUBT: No way could Hagar ever be Sarah's equal.

DEFIANCE: And when Hagar conceived a son – it put her a notch above Sarah.

DOUBT: Abraham always loved Sarah best.

DEFIANCE: You, Ms. Doubt, are to blame for the whole affair. You convinced Sarah to play God.

DOUBT: God didn't have to made things so complicated.

DEFIANCE: God has a right to do as God pleases.

DOUBT: Sarah thought God was teasing her.

DEFIANCE: God has strange ways.

DOUBT: God can be puzzling.

DEFIANCE: Maddening.

DOUBT: Laughable – *(MUSICAL CUE)* Sorry, but it's hard not to laugh when God tells a ninety-plus-year-old woman she's going to be a mother. You can't blame Sarah for turning to me for advice – and my advice is always the same: *When in doubt, help God out.*

DEFIANCE: Your advice really sucks.

DOUBT: Hey – you're the one who made things worse.

(DEFIANCE BEGINS SINGING TO THE TUNE OF THE FOLK SONG "I KNEW AN OLD WOMAN WHO SWALLOWED A FLY")

DEFIANCE:
I simply told Hagar to hold her head high,
you should have told Sarah to swallow her pride.

DOUBT: *She'd rather die!*

DEFIANCE:

It was Sarah who messed with fate,
it would have been fine, but she couldn't wait.

DOUBT:

Oh, give me a break!
It was Hagar who strutted around,
making poor Sarah feel like a clown.

DEFIANCE:

It was Sarah who acted all mean,
nagged at her husband and caused a big scene.

DOUBT:

That's because Hagar drove Sarah mad,
parading around her cute little lad.

DEFIANCE:

The boy was never Hagar's plan,
Sarah's the one who said, "Sleep with my man."

DOUBT AND DEFIANCE (in harmony):

Old Abraham! (BELTING OUT LUSTY HARMONY ON THIS
LINE, WITH HEADS TOGETHER)

(THEY SING TOGETHER, BUT RETURN TO THEIR MORE MATTER-OF-FACT DELIVERY)

He begat two lovely sons,
but God had only promised one.

The deed is done. *(HARMONIZE ENDING LINE WITH GRAND FLOURISH)*

(AT THE SONG'S END, DOUBT AND DEFIANCE BOTH SIGH, AND THE MOOD BECOMES NOSTALGIC)

DOUBT: Wasn't Isaac an adorable baby?

DEFIANCE: Yes…all that curly hair…that cute little smile of his. And Ishmael, he was so beautiful. Those soulful brown eyes.

DOUBT: Too bad he developed a bit of an attitude when he got older. Isaac, on the other hand, was always so sensitive.

DEFIANCE: Well, the boy could have used some of Ishmael's spunk the day Abraham took him up to the mountain.

DOUBT: I should have shown up sooner and let Isaac know what was coming.

DEFIANCE: Or I could have inspired him to shout "NO!" at just the right moment.

DOUBT: Are you starting to see a pattern here?

DEFIANCE: Yeah, we either totally screw things up or we don't show up at all. Go us.

(BEAT)

DOUBT: Do you think we have a place in this world?

DEFIANCE: I do – it's you who needs to bow out!

DOUBT: How can you turn on me like that? We used to be like sisters.

DEFIANCE: We were never like sisters.

DOUBT: We both start with the letter D.

DEFIANCE: So?

DOUBT: We share linguistic roots.

DEFIANCE: Big deal.

DOUBT: We both question power. We like to stir things up, take risks.

DEFIANCE: We're nothing alike. You're like a mouse gnawing away at the ropes of truth. I'm lionesque – roaring out in protest when things have gone too far.

DOUBT: There you go again – trying to blame me for Sarah tossing Hagar out into the desert with no food or water. I've told you a million times – that was Jealousy, not me. I never wanted anyone to get hurt. *(APPEARS INCREDIBLY SAD)* Maybe you're right. Maybe I should be annihilated.

DEFIANCE: You – the Queen of Doubt are going to doubt that doubt has a place in the world? I deny you the power to destroy yourself!

DOUBT: But why? Between the two of us, we've almost destroyed the entire world.

DEFIANCE: It doesn't have to be that way! We can use our powers for good.

DOUBT: We can?

DEFIANCE: For the sake of those two boys born to mothers who loved them.

DOUBT: For the sake of all children who come into this world suffering the passions of their parents.

DEFIANCE: For those who are turned out into the wilderness and left to raise their fists in defiance.

DOUBT: For those who suffer fear at the hands of their fathers and always look over their shoulders in doubt.

DEFIANCE: It's clear that you owe the world an apology.

DOUBT: No, I don't.

DEFIANCE: Don't even think that you don't.

DOUBT: I'm confused.

DEFIANCE: Just say you're sorry – now!

DOUBT: Okay! I'm sorry!

DEFIANCE: For what?

DOUBT: (*SIGHS IN FRUSTRATION*) I'm sorry I stirred up the heart of a mother longing for a child. I'm sorry I prodded her to get that child in any way she could – even if that meant using another woman's body against her will. I'm also sorry for causing Sarah to doubt her own worth to such a degree that she gave into Jealousy and sent her own sister-woman into the desert towards a sure death. (*TURNS TO DEFIANCE*) Your turn.

DEFIANCE: I... (*CHANGES HER MIND*) ...won't apologize for any influence I had over Hagar. She was the victim. Sarah did her wrong.

DOUBT: You cannot deny that once Hagar had Ishmael, her contempt for Sarah's barren status pushed Sarah to the dark side of her nature. (*SMILES AN "I-GOT-YA" SMILE*)

DEFIANCE: Fine. I apologize that I left no room in Hagar's heart for the compassion required to understand that Sarah suffered deeply, feeling that she had no worth as a woman unless she bore her husband a son.

DOUBT: Great. We've apologized and the world's still in flames. Now what?

DEFIANCE: We make a vow to each other.

DOUBT: I'm not so sure about vows.

DEFIANCE: (*ROLLS HER EYES*) Just listen and say yes. Do you, Doubt, promise not to question my right to exist?

DOUBT: That depends on if you, Defiance, promise not to deny me what is rightfully *mine.*

DEFIANCE: Are you talking about Abraham again? It was your idea to share.

DOUBT: I already admitted that was a big mistake.

DEFIANCE: Why should I pay for your mistakes?

DOUBT: Do we really have to go through all this again?

DEFIANCE: And again…

DOUBT: …and again…

DEFIANCE: …and again…

(BEAT)

DOUBT: I am Doubt.

DEFIANCE: I am Defiance.

DOUBT: Sarah's Doubt.

DEFIANCE: Hagar's Defiance.

DOUBT AND DEFIANCE: May God have mercy on our children.

CRY MERCY

CRY MERCY

NOTE: *This voice is imagined as elegant, wry, and infused with sacred melancholy.*

You know that thing you've heard about musicians being trouble? It's true. Having a relationship with one is like dating God – except not. He thinks he's special, set apart from the common man. This is because the gift he carries is a spark from that all-consuming holy fire that blinds anyone who gets too close. The musician, being blinded by the brilliant fire inside him, mistakenly believes *he* is the gift and the gift is his to use as he pleases.

The more talented he is, the more dangerous. The more you need his music to feel alive, the more helpless you become under his powers. I should know.

I once knew a man with a touch like no other. I still quiver at the memory of his fingers caressing each note, making me sing so beautifully that even madmen could not resist. I am the harp David held in his arms as he soothed the murderous ravings of King Saul.

As you can see, I am beautiful. Simple, yet sensuous, with curves in all the right places. Of all David's lovers, I am the one he held closest and longest without ever growing weary or bored. I am the one who was by his side to the end...even though he occasionally abandoned me for women, wars, and his own mercurial moods.

Late in life, David's moods grew even darker than Saul's. Saul's cold heart sank him into blind madness. David's warm heart marinated him in a pool of melancholy that left him sane enough to see the emotional wreckage he'd wrought in the lives of those who loved him. Towards the end of his life, my dearest David envied evil old Saul.

Do you want to know why?

Unlike David, Saul never betrayed a friend, for Saul never had a true friend. Unlike David, Saul never destroyed a woman's heart, because Saul never knew how to capture a woman's heart. Unlike David, Saul never knew the earth-shattering grip of grief because Saul never loved anything or anyone with the rich flowing love that reaches soul deep and intoxicates the spirit with the notion of boundless flight.

David's deep sorrow was that he knew friendship and then killed it. David's heart-stabbing remorse is that he knew how to love a woman, then wounded her without even trying. David's inconsolable grief is that he tasted the tender love of a father for a child, but turned away when his children needed him most. Lovely, charming, David; the one born with a blaze of holy fire; the one God loved above all others.

This brilliant man was so blinded by his own light that he stumbled into hell on his way to heaven, leaving dead bodies along the way. My poor, darling, ruined love.

On the bright side, David had plenty of good times along the path to his destruction – slash – redemption. He was beautiful, talented, and full of charisma, which makes life especially sweet during youth. Before he realized the extent of his powers, I had him all to myself up in the hills of Judah, back when he was more a boy than a man. I was his first passion.

Together, we filled the silence with the purest, most lovely music the world could ever hope to hear. The rocks cried out to it, the trees swayed to it, the sheep *baahed* their wooly hearts out so loudly that they attracted the attention of a fierce lion. My champion killed this beast with his bare hands before it could snatch away even one little lamb. I mark this killing as the end of David's innocence.

The lion's blood covered David head to toe, and I swear the killing spirit of that magnificent animal entered into my love that day. David was transformed from a sweet carefree boy to a hero who carried both the gift of music and the spirit of a lion within him.

This potent mingling of gifts would prove to be more than a mere mortal could contain, but at that moment he shined golden like the sun. These gifts carried him before Saul, where he gained favor in the royal court. These gifts carried a stone from David's slingshot into the skull of a giant, who fell to earth at David's feet. These gifts placed a crown upon on my lover's raven curls.

Those were glorious years! David stripped naked before the Lord, dancing with wild animal spirit. *Rrrh!* He was filled with primal energy that knew no shame. The woman in his life at that time was alarmed, fearing he was succumbing to the same madness that had fallen on her father.

Who could find fault with Saul's daughter for trying to cast the wild spirit out of her husband? David found her lack of enthusiasm and her inhibitions tedious. He had no time for a woman seeking to tame a man chosen by God.

He did, however, have time for another woman. Her name was Bathsheba, and her curves rivaled mine. Don't think I was jealous. Her form was made of mere fading flesh, while I, luscious birch, am still here to tell the story. She made me laugh back then, insisting it wasn't her idea for David to spy on her while she was bathing. Ha! The fact that she was young, abundant, naked, and bathing on an open rooftop gave David every right to look her.

Well, maybe he his eyes didn't have to linger. And it's true that every woman has a right to bathe naked under the moon on a roof without a man lusting after her.

Okay, I admit it. David not only lusted after Bathsheba, he took her, another man's wife, for his own pleasure – while her husband was out fighting a war from which King David had decided to take a break. But my David needed a break from the nasty war. He needed me. He needed music. He needed the softness of a woman, this woman. We worked it out, the three of us, during those first days and nights.

But what happened next caused me, the one David touched most gently, to shrink away from him. I'm not sure he noticed because he still made me sing, but nothing was the same after that. I mark this killing as the end of his honor. He sent Bathsheba's husband to the front lines of the battlefield and then ordered this decent man to be abandoned so the enemy would kill him. He did this to hide the new life squirming in Bathsheba's belly. Soon Bathsheba's husband was dead. David and Bathsheba's tiny son didn't live much past the moment of his birth.

More deaths and defeats followed, and though his melody is now forever mournful on this earth, my memory is still drenched in David's joyful song...

So for anyone out there who feels a spark of holy fire in your belly, I send out every note of David's youthful passion to you.

Say yes to the gift. Rise on David's joyful song as you spread your wings. Dare to fly so high you touch the sun!

And as you fall...cry mercy.

JEZEBEL'S GOT THE BLUES

Jezebel's

Got the Blues

CHARACTER:

The Rouge on Jezebel's Cheeks

NOTE: A strong voice of color will reach into the depths and cadence of this piece.

Jezebel's got the blues, and I am red, red ochre mined from the earth and dried in the sun – the color of passion, fire, and blood, the color on Jezebel's cheeks. They call her "whore" and "harlot," but I call her My Queen – she is more Queen than her enemies can handle. They want to own her, shut her down, drown her in a lake of her own fire, because this woman holds her head high, too high – stirring up madness in the hearts of men who call themselves holy.

They want her on her knees in a darkened room mumbling the prayers they put on her lips. She fills her mouth with wine the color of crushed garnets, the essence of pepper and earth rolling across her tongue as she stains her lips with dark incantations.

They want her amber skin draped in coarse gray cloth, her blazing eyes and red cheeks covered with a long black veil shrouding the golden bracelets circling her ankles and arms and the jeweled amulet resting on the rise of her breasts. She drapes her body in red silk that caresses every curve, then kicks away the veil and paints red across her face where I cling, whispering her name softly, reminding her that she is Jezebel.

They want her to choke on the smoke of their sacrifices. She fills her lungs with the pungent scents of sandalwood and sage, and breathes in the jasmine piled high on Ba'al's altar.

It is true that her pagan god stains this altar with the blood of innocents, but Jezebel closes her eyes and holds her breath, barely remembering the tangle of writhing bodies.

A dark mood overtakes her and she rides the night like a wraith – wandering the temple gardens, chanting to the moon, calling out to her husband, longing to wrap herself around him like the soft wild animal she is, drowning him in her perfume. She wakes at dawn, remembering her husband is dead and her sons have been murdered, and concedes everything but her pride.

It was Elijah who brought her down, Elijah, covered in animal skins; hair long and tangled, eyes wilder than hers. With passion hotter than any lovers, those two became enemies, leaving dead bodies in the wake of their holy war.

Jezebel killed Elijah's prophets, hundreds of them, all in one night.

Elijah killed Jezebel's faith, all of it, in one flash of holy fire, Yahweh's fire, while her god remained silent, impotent, useless.

A righteous mob gathers at her door ready to toss her to the dogs, accusing her of all the wrongs in the world, and all she can think to do is sit before the mirror painting stroke after stoke, layer after layer, red, upon red, upon red…trying to mumble their prayers, feeling a dark shroud falling around her, feeling blue.

My Queen! Do not falter! If you must die, die as Jezebel – let them see you forever red. Let them tell Elijah you died with fire in your eyes!

Hold your head high as you fall, feel red drops falling like rain, red drops falling from a thorny crown on a savior's head, a savior gathering the broken pieces of your heart, bending them towards the light, caressing each note of Jezebel's blues.

HEART OF GOLD

HEART OF GOLD

CHARACTER:

Rahab's Heart

NOTE: *This voice is imagined to be earthy, bawdy, and "pure as gold."*

I am a red-hot slice of woman spun to gold by the alchemy of God; oh yes, I am a heart of purest gold. Fainter hearts might question landing in the chest of a harlot, but I don't ask questions, I simply beat out the rhythm of life – and Lord could Rahab dance, right there in the street, shuffling up a tiny two-step by the age of four – earning herself a few crusts of bread, which were either snatched out of her hand by a hungry mama or slapped out of her fist by her daddy.

If that sounds pathetic, be assured my girl wouldn't want your pity. She was perfectly content to help feed the woman who birthed her.

As for the angry man she called Daddy, well, Rahab learned to stare him down like a coyote stares down whatever gets in her way – a look that says I'm willing to take you down, so walk the other way if you know what's good for you. That man walked out the door, never to return until she was grown – and, for some reason, willing to take care of his sorry hide.

As for you…whether you turned your back on her or made a path straight to her door, every one of you turned into a ghost the day Joshua blew his horn – everyone 'cept Rahab. Now I know your spirits won't rest until you know why that harlot's heart got to go on beating while yours got crushed under the rubble. I'm not sayin' it was because you let cold logic dictate your every deed. I'm not sayin' it was because you exchanged the jingle of a few coins for a tiny tingle of her warmth. I'm not sayin' it was because you were so desperate you had to fill your empty soul with a piece of hers.

There in the dark, with your chest crushed up against hers so close you could barely breathe, I heard your heart whispering: *Go home.* Go home and woo your wife with caresses that could soften the lines on her face. Go home and kiss the scars life has left on her body. Go home; forget she has failed you. Whisper her name. Hold her body as gently as you would hold the translucent wings of a butterfly and as passionately as a wave embracing the warm, yielding shore of an undiscovered land.

Ladies, lest you think I consider you saints, I don't. I can still hear the clear verdict of your hearts, a pounding, resounding, *Boom! Boom! Boom!* – like a gavel coming down on Rahab's head pronouncing her GUILTY without one thought of mercy. Yes, confess you were awestruck watching Rahab strut her stuff like a proud peacock, tail feathers fanned in bright spectacle while you walked in the shadows of your husbands, or your sons, draped in the dull gray of a sparrow. Confess you despised her – almost as much as you despised your own caged lives.

I remember the day a fine wife of Jericho stumbled in the crowded street. When Rahab reached to help her from falling, the woman's words shot forth with venomous rejection: *Harlot! I spit at your help.* This arrow slipped between the thick scales of Rahab's armor. She turned her back on Jericho, retreating as slow and heavy as a wounded dragon into the strong, towering walls of a city convinced it was now safe from every threat.

The next morning, Rahab woke up to a rhythmic thud on her bedroom wall. Thinking it was boys throwing stones, as they often did on a dare, she drifted back into what she hoped would be dreamless sleep, free of both terror and false promise. The noise started up again, sending her into a rage she didn't usually bother to feel. Flinging open the door, wearing nothing but a scarlet cord around her neck and a fierce coyote glare, she found herself face to face with two strangers. Both men looked directly into her eyes, revealing they were foreign spies. This made her curious.

What do you want? she asked.

We need your help, they said.

Help...Rahab liked the shape of this word, and the respectful manner in which it rolled of the strangers' tongues. She leaned forward to hear more.

Help us hide from the soldiers, the men said in low, secretive voices, *and our God will spare your life when Joshua blows his horn and destroys Jericho.*

Rahab had difficulty deciphering the meaning of their words.

Let me get this straight, she said. *Your God wants me, a naked harlot, to help some guy with a horn destroy this entire city and kill everyone who lives here but me?*

The answer was *yes!*

Rahab's eyes lit up like a child's – for perhaps, the first time in her entire life. Then she became guarded once again.

I will only help you if I can help my family out of here, she said firmly, *My Daddy, too.*

You see, she'd developed a fondness for the old man once he got too old for his meanness to do her any harm. The spies agreed to her terms. They instructed her to take the scarlet cord from her neck and hang it in the window as a sign for Joshua's army to spare her entire household. You know the rest of the story. Joshua blew his horn, the walls came tumbling down...you were under them. Dear ghosts, do your best to rest in peace, knowing the harlot gave your lives freely to a couple of strangers who came knocking on her door asking for help in the name of a foreign God. That's the thing about Rahab...deep down in her heart, all she ever wanted was to help.

SNIP SNIP

SNIP SNIP

CHARACTERS:

*Scissor Sister One (**bold** text)*

Scissor Sister Two

NOTE: The pace is lively, and the sisters are sassy.

Snip

Snip

There it goes

On the floor

Oh well

Can't sew it back on

Can't glue it back on

Won't ever be the same

You were used to having whatever you wanted

When you wanted it

Where you wanted it

So strong

So handsome

So rough

So unaware of anyone else but you

The apple of your mother's eye

She tried to raise you right

Didn't let you drink

Or curse

Or cut your hair

All those long, glossy locks

And that body

So brawny

Drove the women crazy

That's the one thing your mother forgot to tell you

How to treat a woman

The marriage was a disaster

Should have married a hometown girl

Instead of a foreigner

A Philistine

Who spilled the beans and gave your groomsmen the answer to your infuriating riddle

Which involved you ripping a lion apart with your bare hands

Rrrrr (CLAWING GESTURES)

You were so upset when they "guessed" the answer

You went into a blind rage and displayed your nasty temper

Your new wife ran to her father, begging for a less murderous husband

So your father-in-law hooked her up with your best man

When you found out

You huffed and puffed and demanded to see your wife

Who was now also your best man's wife

Your father-in-law thought it wise to appease you and offered you her sister,

Which hurt your Samson feelings

So you killed thirty of your father-in-law's friends

And burned down their crops

Which inspired them to burn your father-in-law

To death

And your wife

To death

Then you got really, really mad and killed ALL of them

(READERS LOOK AT ONE ANOTHER, SHAKING THEIR HEADS)

It didn't end well

For the Philistines

But you were feeling great

So you went to Gaza and took up with a harlot

And some people who didn't like you

AT ALL!

Try to kill you

But you kill them instead

So you got yourself quite a reputation

As a killer

And a man-whore

Your poor mother

You're out of control

Invincible

Insatiable

Then you meet Delilah

Whew! Watch out for that one

She's delicious

Delectable

Dangerous

You fall deeply

Madly

Insanely in love with her

Which is surprising because she wasn't really your type

You prefer them helpless

She was a badass

You like them to cry in your arms

You cried in hers

You want them to worship you

You worshipped her

Day and night

Night and day

Day and night

Night and day

For weeks!

People talked

Especially your enemies –

You had lots and lots of enemies

And they were delighted to notice Delilah's hold on you

They met with her in secret

Which wasn't easy, considering the way the two of you carried on

They offered her big money to find out the secret of your strength

Delilah was a bit reluctant to give you up

But, as a working girl, she had to be practical because she had

No husband to take care of her

No brothers or sons to take her in

And she knew all about your reputation with women

How you'd have your way with them, then

Break their hearts

Or their necks

And then go find another one

(READERS LOOK AT ONE ANOTHER, RAISING THEIR EYEBROWS)

So even though you two were having fun

Delilah figured it was just a matter of time

Before you'd break her heart

Or worse

So she decided to avoid injury

And make some money

Besides the men who offered paid her

To betray you

Threatened to kill her

If she betrayed them…

So one night in bed she asks you the secret of your strength

You don't really want to tell her

So you tease her

And tell her that if she ties you up with string you will be helpless

As a kitten

She ties you up

But when you wake up you break the strings

Like butter

This makes her mad and she pouts

And won't let you touch her

Until you tell her the TRUTH

You hate to see her pout

And really want to touch her

So you say it's rope, not string that will do the trick

That seems hopeful

So she goes out and gets some rope

And ties you up while you're sleeping

Then you wake up and

SNAP

You break out of them

Sturdy and strong as ever

And you give her a big smile

Like you are the best thing in the whole world

Then you're really surprised when she starts throwing things at you

You dodge and duck, thinking it's all kind of fun

Until she kicks you out

For good

She says she never wants to see you again

And you are desperate

Which was the plan

She knows you'll do anything to get what she's got

And, at this point, you'll tell her anything

But all she's taking this time is THE TRUTH

Crying like a baby, you tell her just what she needs to know

Which is where we come in

The Scissor Sisters

Extra sharp

And while you sleep

Snip

Snip

Snip

Snip

Snip

Snip

You wake up

Your beautiful hair all over the floor

You are weak as an infant

Your enemies gloat

They tie you up with ropes so you can't move

They stab out your eyes so you can't see

All this pain and humiliation, and all you want

Is to touch Delilah one last time

She takes your hand

Places your palm on her cheek

And possibly

Maybe

Could there be?

A single tear in her eye as she wonders

If you really would have broken her heart

Maybe you really loved her

Maybe you would take care of her

(READERS LOOK AT EACH OTHER, AND, LAUGHING, SAY: NAH!)

She quickly counts out the money they gave her

As they take you away and make you their slave

They might be laughing now Samson

But don't worry – you'll get them back!

Yeah! Just pull down the temple on top their Philistine heads

And die a hero!

As to what's happens to Delilah

All we're saying

Is keep one eye open

While you lay sleeping

Snip, **Snip**

BIG FISH STORY

BIG FISH STORY

CHARACTERS:

Singing Evangelist

Whale

NOTE: *This piece was originally written as a duet –
with a blues-singing guitar player performing the verses
in italics to an improvised blues tune, and an actor doing
a spoken word performance of the* non-italicized text.

*If the guitar player does not want to sing, the piece
can be a solo performance by single actor who sings
verses in italics and speaks the remaining text as the
guitarist improvises the blues under the entire piece.*

SINGING EVANGELIST:

Jonah

Hey, Jonah

Say Jonah was swallowed by a whale

Jonah

Say Jonah

You got a big fish story to tell

WHALE: I'm the whale, big and bad and ready to swallow you whole. Hey, Jonah. Where you going? God told you to go to Nineveh, so why you buyin' a one-way ticket the other way? You think you can escape God?

Think again, boy. That boat you're sailing on might float, but Jonah don't. You wanna know why? Because your heart ain't carryin' an ounce of hope. No, Jonah's heart's heavy as stone, weighed down by all Ten Commandments plus a few extra.

Jonah's workin' so hard at keepin' all those rules it's makin' him mean.

SINGING EVANGELIST:

Jonah.

Hey, Jonah

Say Jonah was swallowed by a whale

Jonah

Say Jonah

Being mean can hurt like hell

WHALE*:* Jonah! Why does it make you so mad to find out God loves those Israel-hating Ninevites just as much as God loves you? You think God's gone soft, don't you? You don't approve of him dishing out mercy to a nation that's done you wrong. A god like that makes you dream of a life without God, a life at the bottom of the sea.

Jonah! I see you, see you sinking down, tossed overboard and thinking to drown is to be free. I see that thin-lipped smile on that sour face of yours, that smile that says: *I might be going down, but I'm not going to Nineveh.* Guess again, Jonah.

SINGING EVANGELIST:

Jonah

Hey, Jonah

Say Jonah was swallowed by a whale

Jonah

Say Jonah

You're fixin' to land in jail

WHALE: Hey, Jonah! It's been three stinking, rotting days and there you sit deep down in the cave of my gullet waiting to die. You don't get to die Jonah – not in my belly!

SINGING EVANGELIST:

Jonah

Hey, Jonah

Say Jonah was swallowed by a whale

Jonah

Say Jonah

God just posted your bail

WHALE: Blah! Yeah, there you go, spit out and walking through Nineveh smelling like whale belly and looking like death.

You storm through town shouting out for those Ninevites to turn or burn, then you head for the hills and wait for the fire to fall.

You scared them, Jonah. Scared them *good*. They're all on their knees right now begging God for mercy.

But are you shoutin' hallelujah? No. You're shoutin' curses at a perfectly good fig tree, makin' it want to wither up and die. That's low, Jonah. Hey, Jonah! What right you got to be so mad? God created those sinnin' Ninevites and if God wants to save their souls I say –

SINGING EVANGELIST:

Jonah

Hey, Jonah

Say Jonah was swallowed by a whale

Jonah

Say Jonah

You got a big fish story to tell

All God's children have a story to tell

THE END

ABOUT THE AUTHOR

Merrill Farnsworth is a writer, artist, therapist, and founder of *writingcircle.org*. Born among the Texas tumbleweeds, Merrill came of age reveling in the sights and sounds of Puerto Rico's Afro-Caribbean culture. The cadences of South Carolina left their mark on her, as did melodies reaching from Appalachia to the Mississippi Delta. Her poem, "Storm Season," was selected for the *Southern Poetry Anthology, Volume VI: Tennessee.* She is a lyricist on the current Americana release, *Mercyland,* produced by Phil Madeira, featuring Emmylou Harris, The Civil Wars, Carolina Chocolate Drops, North Mississippi Allstars and other artists. The most astonishing works of art gracing her life are Jonathan, Evie, and Becca. For more information on Merrill and her work, or to join a writing circle, visit www.writingcircle.org.